EUROPA ✠ MILITARIA Nº 5

US MARINE CORPS
IN COLOUR PHOTOGRAPHS

TEXT AND PHOTOS BY

YVES DEBAY

Windrow & Greene

THE USMC TODAY

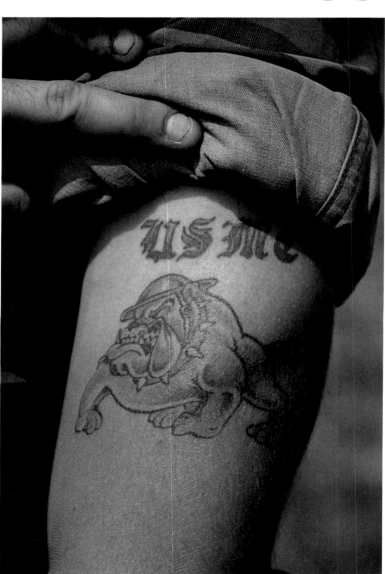

Although administratively dependant on the US Department of the Navy, the US Marine Corps is best considered as a completely separate arm, comparable to the US Army, Navy and Air Force. With a strength of 204,000 the Marine Corps is America's premier intervention force. Its numbers, and its material resources, give the Corps a firepower equal to that of the entire armed forces of a medium-sized power such as Spain, or Belgium and Holland combined.

Though the principal mission of the Corps remains the amphibious assault, it is also prepared for more tightly focused missions: e.g. the rescue of hostages, or the protected evacuation of civilian groups from threatening situations. An 'air/sea bridge' is permanently ready to project the resources of a brigade of Marines anywhere in the world where American interests are involved.

The basic mission of the USMC is to furnish, for the needs of the US Navy, two Fleet Marine Forces: FMF(A) for the Atlantic, and FMF(P) for the Pacific. Together these represent the main combat assets of the USMC, i.e.: three Divisions; three Air Wings; three Force Service Support Groups (logistic units).

The 1st and 3rd Marine Divisions are attached to FMF(P) on the West Coast and on Okinawa; the 2nd Marine Division is an integral part of FMF(A) on the East Coast.

In order to be able to fulfill its basic mission while keeping forces ready at all times for rapid interventions, the Corps has adopted, within the FMF organisation, the principle of tactical groups designated Marine Air Ground Task Forces (MAGTF). These are mixed intervention formations comprising ground and air elements, configured for rapid deployment. This combination of infantry, artillery, armor and air units all integral to the USMC gives the Corps a remarkable flexibility of response; and the MAGTF is assured of support and logistics without having to call upon any of the other armed services.

Apart from combat missions, the crack infantry of the USMC provide part of the presidential guard forces, and protection for US embassies overseas.

A total of 204,000 non-officer personnel serve in the US Marine Corps, and 37,000 recruits are trained each year. All are volunteers signing on for a five-year contract. Additionally, 2,000 officers are commissioned each year on graduation from the academy at Quantico near Washington. The USMC represents some 9% of the total armed forces of the United States.

In 1977 the USMC abandoned the separate career structure which had governed the service of women in the Corps for 34 years; henceforward men and women would serve in the USMC under the same chain of command.

The first women to be authorised to serve in the Marines in fact entered the Corps as early as 1918; they were christened 'Marinettes', and their service ended with the Allied victory. During World War II more than 19,000 women joined for the duration; but it was 1948 before women were able to make the Corps their career. Today there are some 9,700 female Marines of all ranks.

American law forbids the service of women on combat ships, or in tanks and other vehicles serving in the front lines. The women Marines are assigned largely to administrative tasks; nevertheless, they must pass through 'Boot Camp' like any other Marines, and one has been specially created for them at Parris Island. Their training lasts 11 weeks, and is psychologically as hard as that endured by their male comrades. Successful enlistees are sent, according to need, to various training schools to acquire the different administrative, medical or logistic skills. Many women serve in the maintenance crews for Harrier jets at Cherry Point base.

THE MEN AND WOMEN

(Above) Drill Instructors at Boot Camp mould the future generations of Marines. This DI at San Diego wears the 'Montana Peak' hat, the proudly-worn mark of an instructor.

(Left) Although they are not attached to front line combat units, women Marines go through Boot Camp and live firing practice like the men — here, an M60A1 at Camp Pendleton in California.

(Opposite) Wearing the 'Fritz' Kevlar helmet, this Leatherneck with red eyes and camouflaged face prepares to disembark in the Bay of Saros in Turkey during Operation 'Display Determination'.

BOOT CAMP:

ELEVEN WEEKS OF HELL

Each year 37,000 recruits are trained in two large Marine Corps Recruit Depots: at Parris Island, North Carolina, and San Diego, California. Several weeks before their reception would-be volunteers – as in every army in the world – undergo physical aptitude tests and a searching medical examination.

On arrival at Parris Island or San Diego recruits are divided into 50-man squads. Each squad is taken in charge by four Drill Instructors commanded by a Senior Drill Instructor. For 11 long weeks they put the recruits through a punishing ordeal, while instilling in them the rudiments of the soldier's trade.

First of all the recruits are shaved almost bald, and issued fatigues which do not yet carry the famous 'USMC' stencil. Officers address them as 'Private' or 'Recruit'; but the DIs give them traditional nicknames – 'Suzuki' for a Japanese-American, 'Alien' for a boy with big teeth, 'Snow White' for a black, etc.

The 11 weeks' training is broken into three phases which might be described as 'rough hewing', basic shaping, and polishing.

While the purely physical training, though very intensive, is comparable to that of crack troops the world over, the psychological aspects of Boot Camp are perhaps uniquely demanding. All individuality is pitilessly repressed; the DIs set out to systematically break down the recruit's civilian personality. For raw young men the first two weeks are appalling. The DIs shout and threaten ceaselessly. The least individual fault immediately brings a collective punishment down on the whole squad. The recruit who commits a fault is blasted with a torrent of face-to-face abuse bellowed from a few inches' range. These first weeks are passed mainly on the sports field, in the class rooms, and in interminable drill sessions on the immense parade ground. The recruits never speak except to answer the DI by shouting *'Aye aye, Sir!'* If the DI is not satisfied with the decibels produced, the whole squad continues to shout itself hoarse until he is.

After the 'rough-hewing', the next three weeks are devoted to drill, to the theoretical study of weapons, and, of course, to continuing physical conditioning. This is the time of 'stinky recruits', so christened by the DIs when their new fatigues inevitably begin to reek of sweat and grease. Quickly, but at the cost of relentless effort, the clumsy recruit is transformed into a very fit young

(Opposite, top) During one of the interminable combat training sessions at San Diego, one of the recruits shows the strain.

(Opposite, bottom) All the recruits' aggression can be released during bayonet training.

(Above) At Boot Camp everything is done at the double. Each squad's flag will be presented to the Senior Drill Instructor by the best recruit during the passing-out ceremony.

(Right) A traditional image: a Boot Camp drill instructor, 'Smokey Hat' pulled well down, lambasts a recruit.

man. At the end of this period he has to pass a swimming test, crossing 50 yards of water in full field equipment with weapon and helmet.

Next come two weeks during which the recruits are taught more sophisticated military skills, firing the M16 rifle, M203 grenade launcher, and SAW and M60 machine guns. Route-marches, night exercises, grenade training, and classes in camouflage technique alternate with tactical exercises and map-reading.

After this phase the third period of Boot Camp commences with ten days' kitchen, barrack and garden fatigues. The final weeks then take the form of a general recapitulation. Combat exercises, obstacle courses and physical competitions follow one another at a hellish pace. By now the squad has become a unified group, every man reacting as one at a second's notice. The relationship with the DI has subtly changed into a sort of complicity; he constantly tries to push them beyond the limit of their resources, and they accept the challenge, shouting back 'Aye aye,, Sir!', or barking 'Haw haw!' – a canine baying adopted by the Marines after discovering that the Germans who faced them at Belleau Wood in 1918 had christened them 'devil dogs'. They will soon be ready for the great day of their graduation ceremony as true 'Leathernecks'.

EXPEDITIONARY FORCES

For overseas expeditionary tasks the Marines' organisation is based on the MAGTF concept. These large formations are made up of various elements according to the particular demands of the mission. The unified MAGTF command can call upon four main elements:

The command element
The ground element
The aviation element
The logistic element

These four components are found in all MAGTFs, but their relative size varies according to the mission. In practice, three different types of MAGTF may be deployed: in ascending order of resources these are the MEU, the MEB and the MEF.

MARINE EXPEDITIONARY UNITS

The MEU is the smallest type of MAGTF, but also the most immediately deployable. One MEU is permanently at sea with FMF(A) and one with FMF(P), usually embarked on five amphibious assault ships and a helicopter carrier.

With a strength of between 2,000 and 3,000

(Below) The 22nd MEU disembarks in the Corsican dawn during the Franco-American exercise 'Phinia 89'.

Marines, the MEU usually comprises an infantry battalion reinforced by a tank squadron; two artillery batteries; a company of LVTP-7 amphibious personnel carriers; and reconnaissance and engineer elements. The air component essentially comprises a strong squadron of 22 helicopters, to which is often added a unit of Harrier AV-8B V/STOL jet fighter-bombers.

The MEU's logistic support group can provide back-up services as diverse as heavy support of engineer or landing units; resupply of ammunition for all types of weapon to units in combat; or even dental care!

The MEU carries 15 days' supplies of all essentials, including ammunition and rations. It may be considered as the precursor, in any given situation, of the arrival of the more substantial MEB.

MARINE EXPEDITIONARY BRIGADES

Commanded by a general officer, the MEB has a strength of anything between 8,000 and 18,000 men. It consists of from two to five regiments of Marine infantry, reinforced by an artillery regi-

ment and by battalion-sized support units. Its air group musters some 70 fixed-wing and 100 rotary-wing aircraft. It can either disembark from ships, or be airlifted, into a bridgehead captured by an MEU; but it is also capable of initiating entirely autonomous operations. The MEB has 30 days' supplies;' at sea it is transported by some 20 ships.

MARINE EXPEDITIONARY FORCES

The MEF, the largest of the MAGTFs, would not be deployed except in the case of a serious conflict, for large-scale operations. In theory the MEF could reach the size of an army corps, and could eventually comprise the total assets of the three Marine Divisions, whose transport would require the requisition of many ships from the merchant fleet. The MEF is capable of conducting autonomous operations for a maximum period of 60 days.

It should be emphasised that the effective strengths and armaments of MAGTFs vary widely, flexibility being the core of the system.

A truck carrying a logistical shelter disembarks in the Bay of Saros. Each Marine unit contains a logistic element.

(Opposite) The LPH-12 *Inchon* of the *Iwo-Jima* class. Helicopter carriers are the basis of all amphibious assaults.

(Left) Around the helicopter carriers are deployed numerous craft to transport both men and material; here the heavy transport ship USS *El Paso*.

(Below left) For getting into a beachhead quickly, nothing beats the 'Spy Rig'. Here LAV crews at Canjuers in the South of France practice a technique used by specialist Marine units (see p.49).

THE AMPHIBIOUS ASSAULT

The *raison d'être* of the USMC is the amphibious assault, and the creation of a coastal beachhead in enemy territory; and the classic role of the Marine is to 'hit the beach' at dawn under naval gunfire and close air support. Things have changed, however, since Guadalcanal, Iwo Jima and Inchon. Modern air-to-surface missiles, sophisticated mines and tactical nuclear weapons forbid the huge concentrations of ships which stood off the beaches of Normandy and the Pacific atolls. Modern means of surveillance and detection, including satellites, rob an invading fleet of any chance of surprise.

In practice, a large-scale amphibious operation is nowadays limited to a powerful raid, which can transform itself into a beachhead for subsequent landings, or into a conquering advance if the initial operation is crowned with success – as in the Falklands operation by the British in 1982. A classical amphibious operation can be undertaken if the enemy has no serious means of resistance, as in Grenada in 1983. Whatever the circumstances, the Marine is trained for the amphibious frontal assault, and to accept any cost in fulfilling his mission.

An MEU is usually transported on five large ships, plus a helicopter carrier of *Tarawa* or *Iwo Jima* class. This flotilla, designated COMPHI-

BROM, comprises (apart from the helicopter carrier) a *Charleston* class LKA heavy cargo vessel; a *Raleigh* or *Austin* class LPD (Landing Platform Deck); a *Thomaston* class LSD (Landing Ship Dock); and two *Newport* class LSTs (Landing Ships Tank). These ships accommodate the Marines, their equipment, and two weeks' supplies of all necessities.

Several days before the landing a site is selected by means of air reconnaissance or satellite photos. SEALs of the US Navy and Marine Recon teams are landed secretly from submarines, Zodiacs, helicopters, or by parachute. They study the enemy's defences and habits, and analyse the suitability of the beaches for armor and heavy equipment. A few hours before the landing they are joined by other specialists such as snipers and 'Anglico' air and artillery fire direction teams.

During the final night the fleet approaches the coast as closely as possible. In the last hours of darkness the LVTP-7s and LCUs (Landing Craft Utility) of the first assault waves are put into the water. At H-10 minutes the LVTP-7s lead the way in under air and gunfire support, to land at first light.

(Above) The US Navy's LCAC hovercraft, the latest means of disembarking troops, is very fast and has a large carrying capacity, but is also very vulnerable.

(Opposite, above) The venerable LCUs still find employment.

(Below) The first assault wave hits the beach at dawn; in wartime the landing zone would have been hammered from both air and sea. To cover their approach the LVTP-7s have put down a smokescreen.

A first wave of seven LVTP-7s is followed within two minutes by a second wave flanked by four M60 'schnorkel' tanks. A secondary landing, or a diversion, can be mounted by a company in ultra-fast Rigid Raider light craft. Meanwhile the helicopter carrier has flown off its first airborne parties, to capture dominating heights or to insert on them Stinger anti-aircraft missile teams, or to seize positions controlling the approaches to the beaches from inland.

Depending upon the terrain and the success of the first waves, within five minutes huge LCAC hovercraft can disembark a platoon of fast, eight-wheeled LAV attack vehicles. Within ten minutes barges and LCACs can be landing more troops and equipment, initially assault pioneers and infantry reinforcements. Within 45 minutes anti-tank vehicles can be ashore; within an hour, mortar batteries; within 75 minutes, artillery . . .

Overhead the helicopters make incessant trips between ship and shore, lifting in the heliborne companies. Two hours after the first boot hits the sand a heliborne artillery battery and its ammunition can be in place in favourable fire positions.

At H + 3 hours, while the Marines work to enlarge the beachhead with the support of Cobras, F-18s and Harriers, the Combat Service Support Element (CSSE) begins to establish its depots on the beach: the Marines' strength depends upon this fantastic logistic capacity. Since the fifth wave the first logistic elements have been coming ashore. At

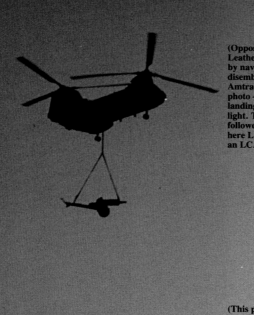

(Opposite) H-Hour! Leathernecks, supported by naval gunfire, disembark from the Amtracs; this is a training photo — in wartime landings are made at first light. They are instantly followed by the first armor: here LAVs disembark from an LCAC.

(This page) Meanwhile, helicopter-borne troops will be inserted into the beachhead, while the second wave of helicopters brings in support artillery. (Right) Marines prepare to board a CH-46 from USS *Iwo Jima* at sea off the French coast during Operation 'Mayflower 90'.

the forward edge of battle there is rarely any shortage of munitions.

During the first hours operations are controlled from a command ship (LCC) of the *Blue Ridge* class, or from the helicopter carrier. Given initial success, the Marines install their command post ashore as soon as possible. They work to prepare an airstrip, improving the terrain to the point where C-130s can begin to land elements of the follow-up MEB.

If the initial attack is checked the Marines will attempt to re-embark – a desperately difficult manoeuvre under enemy fire, but one for which all echelons have trained and practised. In point of fact, only the combination of speed and tremendous firepower can guarantee a successful landing operation.

(Opposite) Reinforcements pour in to support the first waves. During major operations reinforcements come in at the rate of a company every ten minutes.

(Below) Behind the infantry comes the heavy equipment.
(Left) Towed M198 guns arrive at a beach already cleared and marked, while the beachhead is progressively enlarged (right) by infantry supported by M60 tanks.

(Overleaf) Only a few hours after the initial assault the beach is unrecognizable. A jetty allows bigger craft, like the LSTs of the *Newport* class, to unload their tons of material.

THE MARINE DIVISION

(Above) Marines are trained in mechanised warfare in all climates and terrain, from desert to arctic. In the Mojave Desert of California M60s of 1st Marine Tank Bn. support Amtracs used as APCs during a CAX — Combined Armored Exercise.

The division is the largest ground unit of the USMC, which has three active divisions and one reserve. The 1st Marine Division, based at Camp Pendleton in California, and the 3rd, based on Okinawa, are the components of Fleet Marine Force Pacific. The 2nd Division, based at Camp Lejeune, North Carolina, is attached to Fleet Marine Force Atlantic. In time of war the 4th Marine Division would be activated at New Orleans, recalling the Corps' 40,000 reservists. (These reservists undergo frequent periods of refresher training, and are often deployed in formed units within the active divisions – it is not uncommon to see them on duty in Norway or Panama.)

The 12,000-man MARDIV has its own support elements and specialist units. The three infantry regiments represent the bulk of the formation, but the division has three armor battalions (one each of tanks, Amtracs and LAVs), an artillery regiment, a service and an engineer battalion, and the command element. Although not worn on the uniform since the Korean War, the old World War II shoulder patch remains the divisional insignia. Details of divisional organisation are given in the accompanying diagram and order of battle.

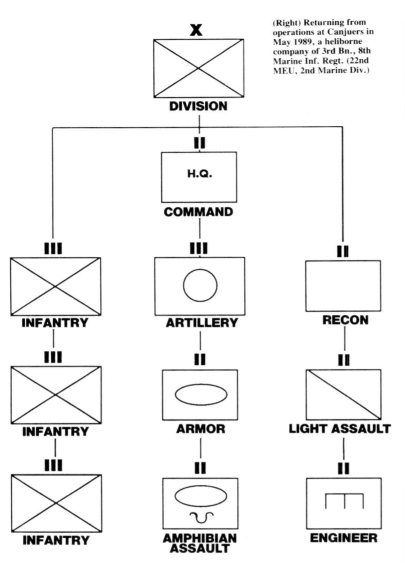

X
DIVISION

II
H.Q.
COMMAND

III
INFANTRY

III
ARTILLERY

II
RECON

III
INFANTRY

II
ARMOR

II
LIGHT ASSAULT

III
INFANTRY

II
AMPHIBIAN ASSAULT

II
ENGINEER

(Right) Returning from operations at Canjuers in May 1989, a heliborne company of 3rd Bn., 8th Marine Inf. Regt. (22nd MEU, 2nd Marine Div.)

1st MARINE DIVISION
(Camp Pendleton, Cal.)

1st Marine Infantry Regt.
5th Marine Infantry Regt.
7th Marine Infantry Regt.
11th Marine Artillery Regt.
1st Marine Reconnaissance Bn.
1st Marine Tank Bn.
1st Amphibian Assault Bn.
1st Marine Engineer Bn.
1st Command Bn.
1st Light Assault Infantry Bn. (LAV)

Units composing the MEUs commited to the Pacific (unit numbers beginning with '1') are drawn from this division.

2nd MARINE DIVISION
(Camp Lejeune, North Carolina)

2nd Marine Infantry Regt.
6th Marine Infantry Regt.
8th Marine Infantry Regt.
1st Marine Artillery Regt.
2nd Marine Reconnaissance Bn.
2nd Marine Tank Bn.
2nd Amphibian Assault Bn.
2nd Marine Engineer Bn.
2nd Command Bn.
2nd Light Assault Infantry Bn. (LAV)

MEUs with numbers beginning with '2' are formed from units drawn from this division.

3rd MARINE DIVISION
(Okinawa)

3rd Marine Infantry Regt. (Hawaii)
4th Marine Infantry Regt.
9th Marine Infantry Regt.
12th Marine Artillery Regt.
3rd Marine Reconnaissance Bn.
3rd Marine Tank Bn. (California)
3rd Amphibian Assault Bn.
3rd Marine Engineer Bn.
3rd Command Bn.
3rd Light Assault Infantry Bn. (LAV)

MEUs with numbers beginning with
'3' are formed from units drawn
from this division.

(Left) Crew of a 'Super Jeep' of 3rd Bn., 8th Marines attached to 22nd MEU during training at Canjuers in 1989. Note the 'Fritz' helmets and flak jackets.

(Opposite) Men of 1/5th Marines in arctic training at Peackle Meadow near Bridgeport, where the temperature can drop to −35° C in blizzard conditions — very different from this 'winter sports' scene.

THE INFANTRY

Above all else, the Marine is an élite infantry-man. After Boot Camp every Leatherneck passes several weeks at either Camp Pendleton or Camp Lejeune learning the finer points of his trade. Before introduction to the mysteries of the laser rangefinder, the Marine has to be able to fight effectively with his bayonet. Recently Gen.Gray, Commandant of the USMC, issued orders that even pilots and logistics personnel undergo infantry combat training several times each year.

In peacetime the three infantry regiments of each division muster three battalions each; a fourth would be added in wartime. The battalion is the basic tactical unit; the MEU is built around one battalion. Battalions are numbered e.g. '1/8 Marines' for 1st Bn., 8th Marine Regiment. Each battalion has three rifle companies, a weapons (i.e. support) company, and an HQ company. Companies are lettered using the international phonetic alphabet, e.g. BRAVO, KILO, LIMA, etc. When deployed as an MEU the battalion acquires a fourth company. As far as practical, battalions try to train their different companies in different specialist skills.

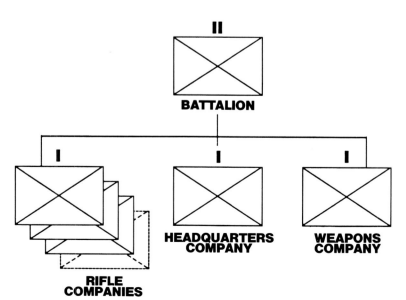

24

THE INFANTRY COMPANY & PLATOON

The Marine infantry rifle company comprises a command group, three rifle platoons and a weapons (support) platoon. The platoon consists of three squads each of 13 men. Each squad, led by a sergeant, is divided into three teams, each of which can produce formidable firepower. The team is led by a corporal armed with an M203 grenade launcher on his M16 rifle. Under his orders are a light machine gunner with a SAW, and two riflemen with M16A2 weapons. Each man also carries one or two AT4 rocket-launchers; this new 'use and throw away' weapon replaces the M72 LAW.

This squad from 1/1st Marines gives an excellent demonstration of the firepower available to the basic 'building block' of the US infantry.

RIFLE
SQUADS

SQUAD

COMPANY

RIFLE
PLATOONS

H.Q.

COMMAND
SQUAD

WEAPONS
PLATOON

MORTAR
SQUAD

3 x 60 mm
M-224

MACHINE
GUN SQUAD

6 x 7,62 mm
M-60 A2

SMAW
SQUAD

6 x
SMAW

PLATOON INDIVIDUAL & COLLECTIVE WEAPONS

M16A2

The basic tool of the Marine is this latest version of the assault rifle introduced during the Vietnam War. At Boot Camp the future Marine learns by heart the name of every part of this rifle, and cherishes it more carefully than his girl. It weighs 7.7lbs, and has an accurate range of 875 yards and an extreme range of 3900 yards. It fires 5.56mm calibre ammunition, from 20- or 30-round magazines, in single shots or fully automatic. It is issued with the M7 bayonet.

M203

This grenade launcher, mounted under the M16, fires a 40mm grenade out to 380 yards. Grenade options include high explosive, canister, illuminating, etc.

M249 SAW
The Squad Automatic Weapon is the American version of the Belgian Minimi. It has a maximum rate of fire of 1000 rpm; is light enough to be carried in the assault; and has three feed options – belts of 5.56mm ammunition, the same magazines as the M16A2 rifle, or 200-round box magazines.

AT-4
An 84mm 'use and throw away' rocket launcher of Swedish design, this can damage, though not destroy, a modern main battle tank at up to 330 yards. It is the infantryman's last-resort weapon against armor, and each Marine can carry two in addition to his personal weapons.

M224 Mortar

(opposite)

Each support platoon has three of these 60mm mortars, giving the company a light, manageable 'pocket artillery'. It can fire up to 20 bombs a minute, and has a crew of two men.

SUPPORT WEAPONS

Each company's single weapons Platoon is divided into machine gun, rocket-launcher and mortar squads.

M60A2 (above)

The standard machine gun since the Vietnam War, the 5.56mm M60 now serves in the modernised A2 version. It is belt fed, and has a rate of 550 rpm and a maximum range of over 4000 yards. The six guns carried by the support platoon provide the company with its base of fire. It can be mounted on a tripod in the sustained fire role.

SMAW (below)

The Shoulder-launched Multi-purpose Assault Weapon, of Israeli design, is used against 'hard targets' such as bunkers, and can destroy light armored vehicles. It weighs just under 17 lbs, and fires an 83mm rocket out to 400+ yards. Each support platoon carries six launchers.

THE WEAPONS COMPANY

The battalion's Weapons Company provides the battalion commander with a considerable integral firepower, to lay down a base of fire during the assault or to stand off armored attack. The company is divided into mortar, machine gun and grenade launcher, and anti-tank missile platoons.

M252 Mortar (left)

The mortar platoon has eight of these 81mm tubes, of British design. The licence-built M252 has largely replaced the old M29, although this is still seen in some units. The M252 has a range of 5km (just over 3 miles).

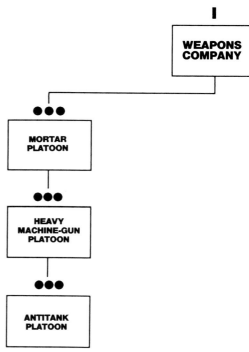

WEAPONS COMPANY

●●● **MORTAR PLATOON**

●●● **HEAVY MACHINE-GUN PLATOON**

●●● **ANTITANK PLATOON**

M2HB Machine Gun (left)

Despite its age, the .50in. 'big fifty' is still in service in the US armed forces, and indeed all over the world; it is unlikely to be replaced in the near future. The machine gun and grenade launcher platoon has six of these classic weapons; it is extremely effective against helicopters and light armoured vehicles.

MK 19 Automatic Grenade Launcher

This 40mm weapon, tried out in Vietnam, fires grenades at a theoretical rate of up to 325 rpm, out to a range of 2400 yards. The machine gun and grenade launcher platoon of the Weapons Company has six launchers.

M47 Dragon

The anti-tank platoon has 24 Dragons, giving an effective anti-armor defence out to a maximum range of 1000 yards. It is a wire-guided missile, steered by the operator by means of a sight mounted on the fibreglass launch tube and electronic impulses passed from his controls down the wire which unreels behind the missile.

To transport heavy weapons the company is equipped with the HMMWV ('High Mobility Multi-Weapons Vehicle', or more colloquially 'Humvee'). Built by Hummer, this vehicle has replaced the Jeep, Dodge and Gamma Goat in the Marine Corps. It is also used as a missile-launcher vehicle, an ambulance, a troop transport, and in various other roles.

SNIPERS

The headquarters company of the Marine battalion includes a small specialist unit designated Surveillance and Target Acquisition Platoon. Its members serve as snipers, trackers, artillery fire direction observers, and under some circumstances as forward air controllers. The sniper is thus the battalion's crack soldier; his speciality number 8541 is only acquired after eight weeks' intensive training.

Kept in reserve for special missions, the STA Platoon may be inserted by helicopter or Rigid Raider into enemy territory, where his marksmanship may disrupt the enemy defence in the early stages of an attack: e.g. by firing on the commanders of approaching tanks, into the embrasures of bunkers, etc.

Much information about the STA Platoons is classified. The snipers work in teams of two, one armed with an M203 and one with an M40 precision rifle or an M16 with modified sights. For street fighting or static work they have a real monster available: the Iver Johnson .50 cal. Special Assignment Rifle. Though its weight of more than 40 lbs limits its deployment, its ammunition is capable of penetrating a substantial wall. The requirement was formulated during the USMC deployment to Beirut.

(Below) A Marine sniper with the monstrous Iver Johnson SAR, which fires the same ammunition as a heavy machine gun and is capable of firing through a wall.

(Above) A sniper armed with the M40 rifle. For the purposes of the photo the camouflage has been lightened but in combat the sniper would be totally invisible from a distance of a few yards.

(Right) The sniper team's observer plays a vital role. This soldier has a sophisticated high-magnification scope; depending upon the particular mission, he can also carry out rudimentary artillery direction and forward air control.

RIGID RAIDERS

The Rigid Raider company is one of the Corps' most recent innovations; one of these specialised companies is at present attached to each MEU.

The Rigid Raider is a small boat capable of carrying ten fully equipped men; its principle qualities are a speed of more than 40 knots, and a fantastic radius of operation – up to 250 miles. This makes it ideal for coastal raids. It can be put into the water from a ship staying well outside the range of enemy radar of coastal defences, and its speed gives the company the ability to strike and withdraw before the enemy can react.

The RRC (Rigid Raiding Craft) can also accomplish other missions. During the Gulf crisis many RRCs were deployed to counter the fast boat attacks of Iranian Revolutionary Guards. During the recent exercise 'Dragoon Hammer' in Sardinia a fully equipped company of Marines was put ashore, embarking for an immediate raid in LAVs. As part of the planning for 'over the horizon' assaults now being studied by the USMC, the Rigid Raider units could mount important diversionary attacks on the flanks of the main landing zones.

Rigid Raider craft; note the two big outboard motors. Background: Foreign Legionnaires who trained with Kilo Co., 3/8th Marines during Operation 'Phinia 89' in Corsica.

A flotilla of Rigid Raiders storm towards the beach. These specialist troops are trained to hit the target and be back out to sea before the enemy can react.

Organisation

The company specialising in RRC deployment is composed, conventionally, of three rifle platoons and a weapons platoon, totalling some 160 men. A small specialist team of engineers and a Dragon AT missile team is added for Rigid Raider operations. The MEU has 20 Rigid Raiding Craft at its disposal.

(Right) The crucial moment in an amphibious assault: the boats hit the shore and the Marines hit the beach.

HELICOPTER SQUADRONS

If the French can claim to have been the first to develop a doctrine for the use of helicopter-borne assault troops during the Algerian War, the US Marines can boast an overall experience of rotary-wing craft going back to Korea in 1952. Helicopters have played their part in all USMC operations since that date. Today, the aerial and amphibious assault operations of the Corps are inseparable; the heliborne attack is launched in parallel with the beach assault. Although the helicopter squadrons strictly speaking form part of the Marine Air Wings attached to the FMFs, we include them with the ground forces with which they principally operate.

The Marine Air Groups (MAGs) in which the helicopter squadrons are organised form part of the three Marine Air Wings (MAWs) attached to the Fleet Marine Forces. The Marine Corps has about 600 helicopters in total. The squadron designations indicate the type of machine operated:

HMM (Helicopter Marine Medium) squadrons have the CH-46 Sea Knight.

HMH (Helicopter Marine Heavy) units have the CH-53 Super Stallion.

HMLA (Helicopter Marine Light Attack) units have the AH-1 Cobra and Bell UH-1N.

The USMC uses four types of helicopter:

CH-46 Sea Knight

The all-purpose workhorse of the USMC, dating from the early stages of the Vietnam War. The twin-rotor CH-46 has a crew of three, and can carry 18 Marines or a slung load of $2\frac{1}{2}$ tons. Its principal mission is heliborne assault; in this role it carries two side-mounted .50 cal. machine guns.

The CH-46 currently used by the Marines has been considerably up-dated, and only resembles the machine of the Vietnam era in basic externals. Among new equipment installed are sophisticated navigation systems, and flare-launchers to divert heat-seeking missiles. Nevertheless, the basic conception and technology remain those of the late 1950s; and the replacement of the Sea Knight by the revolutionary new OV-22 Osprey is awaited eagerly.

CH-53E Super Stallion

The heaviest helicopter in service in the free world, this beast can haul loads of up to 16 tons, which embraces 93% of the Marines' fighting equipment: artillery pieces, LAVs, and all types of personnel and cargo. Equipped for mid-air refuelling and with ultra-sophisticated navigation systems, this giant tri-turbine is surprisingly agile, and can take part in assault landings. It was the CH-53 that was used for the ill-fated American attempt to rescue the Tehran embassy hostages, which came to grief at 'Desert One'.

UH-1N Huey

The descendant of the immortal UH-1H 'Huey' of the Vietnam War, the UH-1N is a modernised twin-turbine model. It is primarily used as a liaison and command aircraft, and for casualty evacuation – it can carry six litters. Nevertheless, it is capable of mounting a GAU2B multi-barrel machine gun and M60 door guns; and if the Cobras are not available, it can be fitted with rocket packs.

HELICOPTERS

AH-1T Cobra

The Cobra, which was blooded in Vietnam, is one of the best weapons in America's arsenal, and has been adopted as the US Marine Corps' support helicopter. A two-seater, with two turbines in its T and W marks, the AH-1 mounts a three-barrelled 20mm cannon; it can also carry TOW anti-tank missiles, 2.75in. rocket launcher clusters, and even AIM-9L Sidewinder air-to-air missiles capable of shooting down most types of hostile aircraft. In the USMC the Cobra serves as effectively in the direct infantry support role as in the anti-tank configuration. For budgetary reasons the Marine Corps has not been offered the UH-64 helicopter adopted by the US Army; but it is currently developing a 'Super Cobra', AH-1W, fitted with the Hellfire anti-tank missile.

THE HELICOPTER ASSAULT

(Opposite) Delivered at dawn, Marines take up combat positions.

(Below) A helicopter-borne company of the 26th MEU prepares to embark during exercises at Canjuers.

A large *Tarawa*-class helicopter carrier can carry 18 CH-46s, six CH-53s and four AH-1s. An *Iwo Jima*-class LPH can take a dozen CH-46s, four CH-53s and four AH-1s. These classes usually carry two Bell UH-1s as well. These LPHs are the 'capital ships' of the MEU, which launch the airborne phase of the assault from the sea. Each

MEU includes two Marine infantry companies specially trained for air assault. In a single wave of 12 CH-46s and four CH-53s, 300 Marines can be helilifted ashore. Their usual objectives are the high ground dominating the landing zone, and road junctions or other choke points on the enemy's reinforcement routes towards the landing zone.

The heliborne company is composed of the conventional three rifle platoons, one weapons platoon and the command element. In the helicopter assault each platoon has a specific task. The first platoon is responsible for the protection of the landing zone. The second platoon covers movements; and the third leads the direct assault on enemy positions.

The weapons platoon of the heliborne company has the usual mix of M60 machine gun, M224 mortar and SMAW squads; but it is also reinforced with two combat teams of six jeeps each, in case the company finds itself isolated behind enemy lines. Two jeeps mount the powerful TOW anti-tank missile launcher, two the 'big fifty' heavy machine gun, and two the automatic grenade launcher.

The vehicles are reinforced examples of the traditional 'Mutt', which are transportable by the CH-53 helicopter; the 'Humvee' is not. In future the heliborne companies will be alone in retaining the jeep.

(Right) A 'Super Jeep' of a helicopter-borne company of the 3/8th Marines at full speed. The personnel are protected by metal roll-bars.

(Overleaf) The heliborne company of the 22nd MEU disembark from their CH-46 of HMM-162 at Canjuers, 1989.

RECON MARINES:
THE ELITE OF THE ELITE

The Recon Marines, easily recognisable by their 'boonie hats', are – as their title indicates – entrusted with reconnaissance operations in the broadest sense. They trace their lineage back to the Scout teams of World War II, who were blooded in the jungles of Guadalcanal. In Vietnam the Recon Marines took part in Operation 'Stingray'; working alone in the jungles flanking the 'Ho Chi Minh Trail', they gathered intelligence on enemy movements, and brought American firepower down on them.

The Recon Marines are currently grouped in three battalions, one per division, and numbered 1 to 3; but they are in practice directly responsible to the two Fleet Marine Forces. Each Recon Battalion has four companies, of which one is the headquarters company. A fourth combat company would be added to each in wartime by mobilising reservists. The company has a command element and three platoons. The platoon has four teams each of four men, and this team is the basic operational element. Normal armament comprises two M16s, one SAW, and a silenced Heckler & Koch MP5 sub-machine gun; but the exact weapons mix depends upon the particular mission, and Recon

Marines are exhaustively trained in the use of many types of foreign weapon.

The Recon team operating behind enemy lines is primarily concerned with avoiding contact so as to maintain its ability to gather intelligence. At any pause on their stealthy march the four members of the close-knit team sink to the ground back to back, one keeping watch in each of the four directions.

Recon teams are trained for insertion by many methods. When carried in by helicopter they may adopt different methods of landing, depending upon terrain and circumstances. Alternatives to the classic rappel are 'fast rope' – a fast slide down a long cable; and, in wooded country, the 'spy rig' – four harnesses all attached to a single winch cable. The Recon Marines, 'Anglicos' and 'Fasts' (see below) are the only Marine units trained for parachute deployment, both static line and free fall, and sometimes jump in from high altitudes.

Infiltration and extraction may equally be accomplished from the sea, by Zodiac, Rigid Raider Craft, or even by submarine. Co-ordinating operations with 'friendly partisans' is also practised. To serve as an ordinary Leatherneck is demanding enough; to be a Recon Marine takes brains as well as muscles, and the highest medical and psychological standards are enforced.

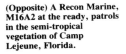

(Opposite) A Recon Marine, M16A2 at the ready, patrols in the semi-tropical vegetation of Camp Lejeune, Florida.

(Below) Men of 2nd Marine Recon Bn. training in the swamps of Florida, near Camp Lejeune. The man nearest the camera is armed with an MP5, a weapon widely used by special forces.

Applicants for this élite force must have served for two years in a Marine battalion before they are allowed to attempt Recon selection training. The first test comes after 15 days of non-stop physical ordeals; if they fail, they have one more week to reach the required standard – and a second failure will send them back to their units.

The Recon Marines are conscious of belonging to a very exclusive 'club' whose other members include such units as the British Royal Marines Special Boat Squadron and the Spanish *Commanfes*. Twice a year they travel to the Philippines, Guiana or Panama for demanding jungle exercises to hone their skills.

A TYPICAL RECON MISSION

Friday: Mission analysis. Objective: to prepare the way for an amphibious operation in Latin America. Briefing, orders, study of satellite photos.
Saturday: Rehearsals, one in morning and a second in afternoon.
Sunday: Final up-date briefing, co-ordination, complete rehearsal.
Monday: Infiltration by submarine, regrouping, surveillance teams take up positions.
Tuesday and Wednesday: Surveillance of enemy.
Thursday: D-Day – main force lands. Exfiltration of teams sent into enemy rear to destroy munitions depot.

Parachute wings, as worn by USMC specialist troops.

(Top and left) Recon Marines must be masters of both water and air as well as land, a mastery achieved only after intensive training.

(Opposite, above) A FAST team returning from patrol near Tank Farm, Panama. Two men are armed with pump-action shotguns, weapons ideally suited to jungle combat.

(Opposite, below) Rapid descent down a 'fast rope' by an ANGLICO team training at Camp Lejeune.

SPECIALIST UNITS

FLEET ANTI-TERRORIST UNITS

One of these company-sized units is attached to each of the two Fleet Marine Forces. The FAST company has six platoons of 54 men. One platoon is always at sea with the duty MEU. The task of these highly specialised units is anti-terrorist operations, e.g. hostage rescue, etc. Their firepower is remarkable; among their mixed range of weaponry is the pump-action Mossberg 500 shotgun.

AIR NAVAL GROUND LIAISON COMPANIES

The ANGLICOs are 'super Marines', trained to be dropped ahead of the advance of the main force to direct supporting fire on to the enemy. These signals specialists can guide a bomber strike, co-ordinate the fire of artillery batteries, or direct naval gunfire from the enormous turrets of the USS *Iowa* or *New Jersey*. ANGLICO teams often operate with Allied marines during multi-national exercises. They may be inserted by parachute, helicopter, submarine or surface craft.

THE LIGHT ARMORED INFANTRY BATTALION

Once the beachhead has been secured the main aim of the MEU commander is to win 'elbow room' for the Marines crowding on to the beaches. The subsequent development of a large-scale operation depends on taking a maximum of territory as quickly as possible. Only helicopters, and the new LAI battalions, are capable of accomplishing this.

Since 1985 the USMC has added to its armory the Light Attack Vehicle (LAV). This eight-wheeled light armored vehicle is a licence-built Swiss Mowag Piranha; highly mobile, and capable of 65 mph on roads, it carries six infantryman and mounts a 25mm 'chain gun'. It is completely amphibious, without preparation.

The LAV fills an important role, and equips the new Light Armored Infantry Battalion created within each Marine Division. Each battalion has three combat companies each equipped with 14 LAV(25)s, and a command element with two LAV(C)s. The battalion's missions include flank protection, fast deep-penetration raids, screening, reconnaissance, pursuit and exploitation; and straightforward support. The battalion also fields a Weapons Company, with 16 LAV(AT)s armed with TOW launchers, eight LAV(M)s mounting 81mm mortars, and eight recce LAVs. The battalion's headquarters company has two command LAVs, three logistics LAVs, and an LAV(R) recovery vehicle. This 'eight-wheeled thoroughbred' gives the Marines an unprecedented capability for fast movement.

```
                    II
              ┌──────────────┐
              │    L.A.I     │
              │  Battalion   │
              └──────┬───────┘
         ┌───────────┼───────────┐
         I           I           I
    ┌─────────┐ ┌─────────┐ ┌──────────┐
    │  L.A.I  │ │  H.Q.   │ │ Weapons  │
    │ Company │ │ Company │ │ Company  │
    └─────────┘ └─────────┘ └──────────┘
```

(Above) Fine portrait of the NCO commanding a LAV (Light Attack Vehicle).

(Opposite) The LAV is a thoroughbred eight-wheeler, which exists in several forms including the anti-tank LAV TOW (above). Below is a standard LAV of 2nd LAI Bn. on the Panama Canal. Vehicles of this unit had their baptism of fire a few weeks later.

THE MARINE TANK BATTALION

At the beginning of the 1973 Yom Kippur War some military pundits were a little hasty in burying the main battle tank as an effective weapon. Despite severe losses in the first days of that conflict, the Israeli Armored Corps later succeeded in opening a road into Africa, and in destroying the enemy missile batteries which had at first denied freedom of the air to Israeli jets.

The US Marine Corps has fielded its own integral tank battalions since World War II, and they have proved their worth in the Pacific, in Korea and in Vietnam. Certainly, the great armored sweeps of a Patton or a Rommel are not realistically credible in the Marines' battle environment; nevertheless, the tanks are indispensable for smashing 'hard targets' at high water mark, for exploiting early success, and for engaging enemy armored counterattacks.

The Marine tankers nearly always take part in the first waves of beach assault in their 'schnorkel' M60s. In the case of operations in desert terrain the 7th MEB would be deployed; trained and equipped for this type of combat, the brigade's M60A1 units would lead the way in conventional armored engagements.

The USMC's main battle tank is the elderly M60A1, massive and imposing. With a four-man crew, a 105mm main gun, one .50in. and one 7.62mm machine gun, the Patton weighs 45 tons and can reach about 32 mph on flat terrain. It is an obsolescent design nowadays, and should soon be replaced by the remarkable M1A1. While awaiting their new mount the Marine tankers have modernised their M60s by adding 'active armor'. These blocks of explosive mounted all over the hull and turret explode if hit by a shaped-charge projectile, diverting its effect from the main armor.

Apart from its four tank companies the USMC Tank Battalion fields a company of Humvees mounting TOW launchers. A reconnaissance Humvee platoon has recently been added to each battalion, with notable success. The command company also has various recovery and bridging tanks.

Each year the three USMC tank battalions spend time at Twenty-Nine Palms, California, for realistic tactical exercises and live firing in the desert terrain.

(Opposite) An M60A1 of the 1st Marine Tank Bn. with active armor. The empty expanses of the Mojave Desert make an ideal training ground.

(Below) Finished in 'Europe No.1' camouflage, an M60A1 exercises in Norway during Operation 'Blue Fox 86'.

In a cloud of dust, M60A1s of the 2nd Marine Tank Bn. pass their colonel's vehicle in review.

MARINE TANK BATTALION

Tank Company

H.Q. Company

Recon Platoon

Antitank Company

THE MARINE ARTILLERY REGIMENT

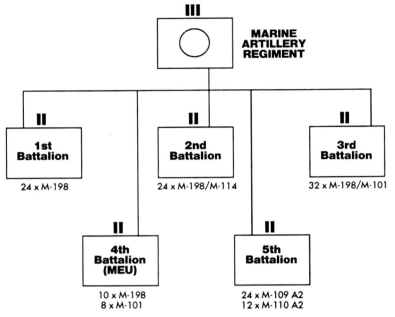

MARINE ARTILLERY REGIMENT

1st Battalion
24 x M-198

2nd Battalion
24 x M-198/M-114

3rd Battalion
32 x M-198/M-101

4th Battalion (MEU)
10 x M-198
8 x M-101

5th Battalion
24 x M-109 A2
12 x M-110 A2

Apart from offshore naval gunfire support, the Marines can count on the fire of the artillery regiment attached to each MARDIV. The Marine Artillery Regiment is a large unit, with a unique organisation and diversity of armament. It is divided into five battalions; each normally comprises four six-gun batteries (except the 4th, which is permanently detached for service with an MEU, and which totals 18 tubes.)

The first four battalions are equipped with towed M101 and M198 howitzers; some remaining M114 155mm howitzers are in the course of replacement by the M198. The 105mm M101 is the Marine gunners' lightest piece, dating from World War II and a veteran of Korea and Vietnam. It can fire in direct support, or lay down barrage fire at a rate of three rounds a minute; its maximum range is 12,000 yards.

The new M198 155mm howitzer is in the course of becoming the USMC's standard artillery piece. Towed by a 5-ton truck, it can be in action within ten minutes. It has a range of 26,000 yards – though that can be boosted to 30,000 ($18\frac{1}{2}$ miles) with

(Left) The helicopter has given greater flexibility to Marine artillery, enabling it to be moved around the battlefield. Here a 105mm M101 of the 26th MEU is already in action as helicopters bring in the rest of the equipment.

(Opposite, below) An M110A2 of the 5/11th Marine Artillery simulates a naval bombardment during a CAX in the Mojave Desert.

(Below) Batteries of M109s were deployed during the same exercise. Firing on fixed lines, these mobile artillery pieces were hidden under camouflage netting.

rocket-assisted ammunition. It can fire four times a minute.

Both these pieces can be heli-lifted by the CH-53, and the M101 by the CH-46. This gives Marine gunners great flexibility; thanks to the helicopter, they can mount 'artillery raids' into the enemy's rear areas.

In all artillery regiments the 5th Bn. is equipped with heavy self-propelled guns for supporting armored and mechanised advances: three batteries of M109 155mm SP howitzers, and two of M110A2 203mm (16in.) SPs capable of firing nuclear ammunition. These heavy SP guns are rarely committed to small-scale landings below the size of an MEB. They often take part in firing exercises, however, either in the Mojave Desert or at Guantanamo base in Cuba.

The new 155mm M198 is the standard artillery piece of the USMC. In spite of its size, it can be slung under a CH-53 (left). The M198 is normally towed, as (top right) in the Bay of Saros, Turkey, during Operation 'Display Determination'. (Below) M198 of the 10th Marine Artillery Regt.

AMTRACS

The first moments of an amphibious operation are crucial. Although the pounding of naval gunfire and tactical air strikes theoretically pulverise the enemy defences, in practice there are always islands of resistance where a few determined men can change the whole course of an operation.

In the early World War II landings the Marines, packed like sardines in open landing craft, simply had to suffer the lash of enemy fire until they reached the beach – and as they charged down the ramp on to the open sand. Later they were transported in armored, tracked 'Alligators' which protected them from all but major direct hits, and could (theoretically) carry them out of the surf and up the beach into cover.

Today the first amphibious assault waves are transported in vehicles developed specifically for this task: the Landing Vehicle Tracked Personnel model 7 – LVTP-7. This large, entirely enclosed, armored, tracked amphibious personnel carrier accommodates 25 fully equipped Marines. It is transported on the large US Navy LPDs, LSDs, LSTs and helicopter carriers, and put into the water one or two hours before the assault. Its very low silhouette in the water, and aluminium armor, protect it during the run in at first light. There are command and recovery versions for the headquarters elements of the amphibious units. Once

on shore its great height and relatively thin armor make it vulnerable to anti-tank weapons; and the USMC are currently developing a new concept, and a new vehicle, for amphibious assaults.

While awaiting the appearance of this new mount at the beginning of the next century under the Advanced Amphibious Assault Program the USMC has up-graded the 18-year-old LVTP-7. The resulting AAV-7A1 (Assault Amphibious Vehicle) has a family resemblance to its predecessor, but many improvements including new transmission and propulsion systems, new anti-shaped-charge side armor, and an automatic fire suppression system. The turret armament has increased to one .50 cal. machine gun and one MK19 automatic grenade launcher. A new version specifically for clearing beach obstacles and mine fields is under development, under the complex designation Catapult Launched Fuel Air Explosive Land Mine Countermeasures Systems (CATFAE).

Each Marine division has an Assault Amphibian Battalion, a large unit with a headquarters company and four combat companies totalling some 200 vehicles, mostly LVTP-7s and AAV-7A1s. An MEU afloat has 15 AAV-7A1s – 12 troop carriers, two command vehicles and a recovery vehicle – and a company of Marine infantry specialising in amphibious assault.

(Above) During Operation 'Anchor Express 86' LVTP-7s, suitably camouflaged, enter the waters of a Norwegian fjord.

(Opposite) An AAV-7A1 creates a 'splash' during Operation 'Phinia 89' in Corsica. The gunner has protected his grenade launchers with a simple plastic bag.

62

THE TECHNICIANS

(Above) During a CAX sappers from the 1st Marine Engineer Bn. advance with live bangalore torpedoes to clear a path through a minefield.

(Left) During Operation 'Phinia 89' in Corsica a bulldozer from the 2nd Marine Engineers unrolls beach matting to stop vehicles sinking into the sand.

(Opposite, top) Anti-aircraft teams equipped with Stingers are attached to the helicopter squadrons. These crews can also contribute to close air defence while still on board the transport ships.

(Opposite, bottom) A photo symbolising the fabulous logistic support available to American troops within a few hours of landing on a hostile beach.

It would be tedious to list – and impossible in this space to adequately explain – all the dozens of specialised trades and skills which the USMC can draw upon in its different training establishments and bases. A modern army on campaign has need of thousands of obscure specialists whose duties are unconnected with the assault proper, but who nevertheless work with an M16 at hand.

Each division has an engineer battalion; these Marine sappers carry out combat pioneer tasks (mine warfare, and the creation or destruction of obstacles) but can also help the US Navy's SeaBees in many of the vital beachhead tasks – e.g., producing 300 litres an hour of drinking water from sea water.

A few hours after the first landing the beach is unrecognisable under an orderly chaos of logistic depots stockpiling every kind of munitions and supplies, and workshops where experts can repair anything from a pack-strap to a helicopter rotor. Once the battle line moves inland a tendency to become domestic, common to soldiers everywhere, soon shows itself in small comforts which appear among tent villages – showers, cookhouses, even cinema screens . . . The MAGTF's logistic unit is as large as the assault units, and as lavishly equipped.

The anti-aircraft defence of the beachhead is assured by batteries of Hawk SAMs, and by teams equipped with the deadly Stinger shoulder-fired missile, the bane of the Soviet Air Force in Afghanistan.

'CHESTY IX'

'Chesty the Ninth', alias 'Theo', is the official mascot of the US Marine Corps. Recently promoted sergeant, this English bulldog delights thousands of spectators at the weekly Friday parade at the Corps' oldest Washington barracks, as he marches in pace and sits down at the word of command.

The first official mascot was 'Mike', an Irish terrier born in 1905, who took part in the 1914 Vera Cruz landings. When he died in 1916 he was buried at Parris Island, where his grave can still be seen. The adoption of bulldogs originated late in the Great War when the Germans nicknamed the Marines 'devil dogs' at the battle of Belleau Wood. US propaganda picked up this compliment, and recruiting posters showed armed and helmeted bulldogs. The first bulldog was 'Jiggs 1', adopted by Gen.Butler at Quantico; he took part in various ceremonies, including flying in a biplane. Just before his death the Department of the Navy promoted him to sergeant-major. Successive generations of mascots have been christened Jiggs, or more recently Chesty, after the much-decorated commander of the 1st Marine Regiment in Korea, Col.Lewis 'Chesty' Puller.

(Above) Portrait of a Marine Corps celebrity, the redoubtable Sergeant Chesty IX.

(Left) The author in Panama during one of his trips with the Marines.

Acknowledgements:
The author wishes to record his sincere gratitude to Cols. Corley and Norako, Assistant Naval Attachés (USMC) at the US Embassy, Paris; to Col. Peck, Chief of Public Relations at the USMC HQ, Washington DC; and to all the officers, NCOs and men who made his job easier on location.

© Yves Debay

Printed in Italy

This edition published in Great Britain 1990 by Windrow & Greene Ltd., 5 Gerrard St., London W1V 7LJ

British Library Cataloguing in Publication Data
Debay, Yves
    US Marine Corps in colour photographs. –
    (Europa-Militaria; 5).
    1. United States. Marine Corps
    I. Title II. Series
    359.960973

ISBN 1-872004-50-4